CONTENTS

• *Glossary terms are emboldened on first use on each spread*

INTRODUCTION

Why do we wear hats? For all sorts of reasons. Hats change the way we look. They frame our face, hide our hair, and cover the most important parts of our body - our brains!

Fashion accessories

Many hats are decorative. We wear them for fun and for fashion. Hats may also tell onlookers about the wearer's sense of style. The wrong hat spoils the smartest outfit, but the right hat helps create the perfect image. Other hats have practical uses. We rely on them to survive.

Status symbols

Hats display people's rank in society. Large hats impress onlookers, and are status symbols. There is an old saying, 'If you want to get ahead, get a hat!' Hats may also reveal the wearer's occupation, and, sometimes their gender. Traditionally, members of different professions wore different styles, and so did men and women. In some societies, a woman's headgear may still show whether she is single, married, or a widow.

Some characters are inseparable from their headgear. US writer Dr Theodore Seuss Geisel created the 'Cat in the Hat' in 1954.

Hats can be used to draw attention to the wearer. This vibrant example here is used by the man to stand out from the crowd.

4

PRETTY IN INK

Religious reasons

Hats can signal religious beliefs or political opinions or group identity. Followers of many faiths, including Muslims, Jews and Sikhs, believe that covering the head shows respect to God. Political campaigners support their cause by choosing hats in their party colours.

Sikhs declare their faith to the world by wearing **turbans**.

How much heat do we lose through our heads if we don't wear hats?

Up to 85%.

Protective clothing

Hoods and headscarves keep our heads warm and dry, or shade us from hot sunshine. Caps, nets and helmets protect us from dirt or danger, the latter particularly in times of war, or while participating in sports such as horseriding or skateboarding.

This man's clothing is designed to protect him from the wind and dust that whips across the Sahara desert.

THE FIRST HEAD COVERINGS

Birds with fine feather crests display them to attract
a mate. Fierce male lions have magnificent manes of hai
Early humans admired these symbols, and copied them
They made headdresses for powerful people.
They hoped these would give their leaders
a share in the wild creatures' power.

The first hats

Archaeologists
do not yet know
when the first hats
were made. But it is
likely that early humans,
over 2 million years ago,
may have draped animal
skins over their heads for
warmth in cold conditions,
or shaded their faces from the
Sun with mats of leaves or grass.

*Animal skins such as
this buffalo hide were
used by early humans
to make simple hats
to keep them warm.*

Traditional headgear

Today, traditional societies in the Amazon rainforest
in South America (right) and the South Pacific still
copy the display methods of animals and birds.
There, rulers and leaders still wear fur or
feather headdresses on ceremonial occasions.

Garlands

In many parts of the world, women and girls still follow another very ancient custom. They thread together beautiful **garlands** of delicate wild flowers to decorate their hair. Flowers called daisies are often used, making beautiful necklaces called daisy chains.

This tribal leader from the Ecuadorian rainforest is wearing a colourful feather headdress, decorated with rainforest flowers.

How do we know that prehistoric people wore flower headdresses?

Traces of flower pollen have been found in prehistoric graves.

It takes patience and nimble fingers to make a daisy-chain.

Fur hats

By 100,000 years ago, men and women had learnt to make tools that could cut furs and animal hide and stitch them together. They made simple tunics and trousers - and, archaeologists believe perhaps, hats as well.

Warm fur hoods, like this one worn by a Inuit from Alaska, may first have been made 100,000 years ago.

In hot, dry, dusty Ancient Egypt, keeping clean was very important. Cleanliness was also a sign of religious purity. Ordinary people washed in the River Nile. Wealthy families had shower rooms, where slaves poured water over bathers standing below.

Cool and clean

For coolness and extra cleanliness, men and women shaved their heads or cut their hair very short. Children had their heads shaved, too, except for a strand left trailing beside one ear. This was called 'the **lock** of youth'.

A wig of curled and braided human hair, made around 1500 BC.

Wigs

Rich men and women wore elaborate wigs made of human or animal hair for fashion, protection from the elements and to cover up baldness. Styles varied over the centuries, from long **ringlets** or thick shoulder-length braids to short, tight curls. On special occasions, wigs might be decorated with beads and scented with perfume. Ordinary people could not afford fancy wigs. They wore rough wigs of plant fibre, or simple lengths of cloth tied round their heads.

What type of hat was depicted in a cave in Thebes?

A conical strew hat.

8

An everyday crown

Ancient Egyptian statues, carvings and tomb-paintings often show **pharaohs** wearing a **pschent** (double crown). This was a symbol of the two separate regions of Egypt, united around 3100 BC. The top of the **crown** was white, representing Upper (southern) Egypt. The lower part was red, signifying Lower (northern) Egypt.

This tomb model shows King Tutankhamun wearing the 'war crown' of the pharaohs.

The sign of a King

Royal crowns and headdresses - **nemes** - were usually decorated with a fierce **uraeus** (rearing cobra). This was the symbol of the goddess Wadjet, a special protector of kings. In neighouring Nubia, rulers wore **diadems** on top of short hair. The diadem featured cobra symbols and two rearing cobra decorations were also placed over the king's forehead.

Left: A bust thought to be of King Amenemhat IV. It shows the pharaoh wearing the 'nemes' headcloth with a uraeus.
Right: Statuette of a Nubian King (7th century BC) showing diadem.

The Ancient Greeks believed that the head was the home of the soul. Greek head coverings displayed the wearer's moral worth, as well as having practical uses. While clothing in ancient Greece was normally a simple linen tunic, hairstyles, particularly for women were very elaborate.

Greek Men

Many Greek men went bare-headed for most of the time. As citizens of democratic states, they felt proud and free, with nothing to hide. When it rained, they wore a **pesatos** (wide **brimmed** leather hat) or pulled their cloaks over their head. Athletes tied their hair back with ribbons, to keep it out of their eyes.

The typical Greek fashion was to go bare-headed for men.

Greek Women

Greek men expected respectable women to cover their hair with veils. Beneath these veils, women arranged their long hair in elaborate braids, curls and buns. Women's hairstyles were held in place by coloured scarves or ribbons, and decorated with jewelled hairpins or **diadems** (headbands).

Ancient Greek jewellers were highly skilled at working with gold.

What was the prize given to the first Olympic champions?

A garland of leaves from holy trees.

A gold diadem to be worn in a woman's hair, from the island of Milos, dated 300 BC.

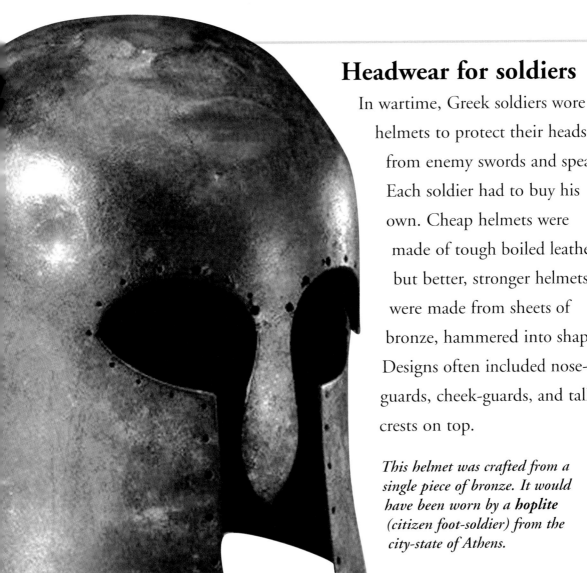

Headwear for soldiers

In wartime, Greek soldiers wore helmets to protect their heads from enemy swords and spears. Each soldier had to buy his own. Cheap helmets were made of tough boiled leather, but better, stronger helmets were made from sheets of bronze, hammered into shape. Designs often included nose-guards, cheek-guards, and tall crests on top.

*This helmet was crafted from a single piece of bronze. It would have been worn by a **hoplite** (citizen foot-soldier) from the city-state of Athens.*

The Sythian Cap

The Sythians were famous archers who acted as a kind of police force in the ancient Greek city of Athens. They wore pointed **caps** with flaps. The caps became fashionable and many other Greek archers copied their style.

This Greek vase painting, made around 500 BC, shows a Scythian archer from Central Asia wearing a pointed cap.

ANCIENT ROMAN EMPIRE

The Ancient Romans inherited many fashions from their neighbours in Greece. But the Romans also followed old Italian customs, and invented new traditions of their own. Late Roman styles were influenced by contact with Germanic and Celtic peoples from north-west Europe from the 3rd century BC. These people had their own typical head coverings and hats.

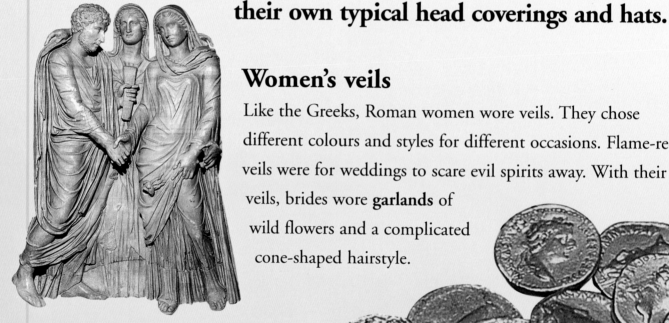

Women's veils

Like the Greeks, Roman women wore veils. They chose different colours and styles for different occasions. Flame-red veils were for weddings to scare evil spirits away. With their veils, brides wore **garlands** of wild flowers and a complicated cone-shaped hairstyle.

A Roman bride with her veil turned back.

Garlands

Roman emperors also wore garlands, but of laurel leaves, not flowers. Roman generals were 'crowned' with laurel as they marched in triumphant processions. Roman writers suggested several reasons for these customs. Laurel represented peace, joy and victory. As an evergreen tree, with leaves all year round,it was a symbol of undying strength. It was sacred to Jupiter, the most powerful Roman god.

Roman coins were stamped with portraits of reigning emperors crowned with aurel leaves.

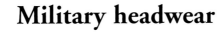

Military headwear

Roman soldiers wore helmets based on Ancient Greek originals, but with many additional features and decorations. Roman helmets worn in battle had adjustable visors, removable cheek-guards and a curved rim at the back of the neck, designed to ward off killer blows. Ceremonial helmets, worn on parade, might be decorated with metals castings or engravings, and have brightly-coloured crests made of feathers or horse-hair.

C 200 BC ~ AD 500

What was marked on the side of a Roman soldier's helmet?

The unit, or division, to which the soldier belonged.

A modern reconstruction of Roman army helmets. Originally, crests helped soldiers identify comrades in battle, and showed rank. After around AD 100, they were mostly decorative.

Conquered peoples

Roman artists often included portraits of conquered peoples in their work. Today, this provides valuable evidence about non-Roman headgear.   For example, Celtic warriors are shown wearing hooded capes, or with bleached, spiky hair; east-Europeans are pictured with close-fitting **caps**. Fair hair, arranged in fantastic styles, was top fashion. Roman women prized wigs made with blonde hair cut from north German or Baltic captives.

Julia Titi, daughter of Titus, shown in an extravagant blond wig.

13

MEDIEVAL EUROPE

After Roman power weakened, soon after AD 300, Roman empire lands were divided among many different peoples. New languages, customs – and designs for headgear evolved. Because different peoples settled in different parts of Europe, their clothing developed into distinctive regional styles.

Visigoth kings hung their glittering crowns in Spanish Christian churches, to give thanks to God.

Visgoths

Around AD 500, **Visigoths** from north-east Europe took control of land in Italy and Spain. They were led by warlike kings, who wore wide, band-shaped **crowns** of gold **lattice-work**, studded with precious stones and with jingling gold pendants. Gradually, circlets of gold and jewels replaced Roman laurel-leaf **garlands** as symbols of royal status in south European lands.

Local headgear

Local climate and farming practices influenced ordinary people's headgear. Married women throughout medieval Europe continued to cover their heads with veils or shawls, but men's hats varied widely. In hot, sunny Italy, for example, men's hats had wide shady **brims**. In cold, snowy lands, like Viking Russia and Scandinavia, men made hats of bushy fox-fur. In wet, windy Britain, they continued to wear Celtic-style hoods.

This Italian farm-worker is wearing a wide-brimmed hat made from locally-grown wheat-straw, plaited then stitched together.

Battle helmets

Men's battle-helmets also reflected local traditions. Viking and Anglo-Saxon helmets, made before AD 1000, were decorated with monsters from pagan myths and legends. Their basic shape was a simple dome, and they were designed to be worn with chain-mail armour. After around 1300, fashions in helmets changed, to suit new styles of plate armour. Metal helmets enclosed the whole head, and had to be individually-tailored.

> The Pope was leader of all Christians in medieval Europe. What was his tall hat called?
>
> A tiara.

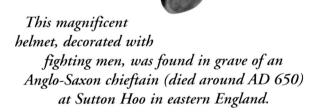

This magnificent helmet, decorated with fighting men, was found in grave of an Anglo-Saxon chieftain (died around AD 650) at Sutton Hoo in eastern England.

Women's hats

Around the same time, rich women began to wear hats, instead of simple veils. At first, their hats were based on male designs. But after around 1400, women's fashions included tall, pointed hennins (steeple-hats), wide, padded hats with horns, and '**gable**' headdresses that formed a pointed frame around the face.

An illustration from a 15th-century Dutch calendar showing women wearing elaborately horned hats.

15

EASTERN REGIONS

Many different peoples of Asia all had their own customs and traditions, which were reflected in their clothes. They lived in many environments, and followed several of the world's great faiths. These factors also affected what they chose to wear.

The traditional Arab keffiyah shades the head and protects the face and neck from sunburn.

Holy headgear

The Muslim faith encourages men and women to dress modestly. Many Muslims believe that this means keeping the head covered in public, at all times. In the Muslim homelands of Western Asia, men wore the traditional desert head covering: a **keffiyah** (square of cotton cloth, folded into a triangle). Muslim women covered their hair with veils or with a fold of their long cloaks, called abayahs. Some also wore a burqa (mask that covered part of the face).

Warm wool and fur

In Central Asia, where the weather was colder and wetter, men and women wore pillbox-shaped woollen **caps**. In winter, men covered their cap with a fur hat, while women tied on a headscarf. Turkish men wore a tall cone-shaped cap of wool felt, called a **tarboosh**. Turkish women kept their heads warm with headscarves and shawls.

A traditional fez, or Tarboosh, worn in Turkey.

Pillboxes and turbans

In many parts of India and South-East Asia, **turbans** (long strips of cloth wound round the head) were the usual headgear or men. Women draped a fold of their ari (wrapped cloth robe) or a long, wide dupatta (headscarf) over their hair. For work in the rice-fields, farmers throughout South-East Asian farmers made shady, waterproof hats of tough local materials, such as bamboo or woven palm-fronds.

Muslim scholars dressed in turbans around AD 1350. Many Muslims and Sikhs still wear turbans today.

China

Chinese hairstyles showed the wearer's rank and occupation. Men grew their hair long, and covered it with a black headscarf. Scholars and government officials topped this with a black hat that had folding side panels; army leaders wore a helmet trimmed with feathers. Farm labourers in southern China wore a wide conical bamboo hat, designed to shed heavy rain. Traditionally, Chinese women tied their long hair into a neat bun. It was not respectable to let it flow free. Outside their home, high-ranking women wore a veil. Clong styles in Japan and Korea were influenced by China, their powerful neighbour. But each country also had traditional headgear and hairstyles of its own.

What is another word for a tarboosh?

A fez.

This model Japanese emperor wears a kammuri (tall black silk hat). His empress has an elaborate suberakashi hairstyle and a chrysanthemum crest.

AFRICA

Traditionally, African men and women wore a wide range of headgear. It was made in different styles and materials, depending on the local environment and resources. African hairstyles followed traditional local designs, each with their own meaning. Typically, styles included braids, hairpins, decorative combs, feathers and coloured clay.

Traditionally, the Tuareg men of Morocco wore veils dyed deep blue with indigo. In Sudan, white veils were popular.

Dressed for the desert

Men and women living in or around the vast, sandy Sahara Desert needed headgear that would protect them from heat, dust, sandstorms and sunburn. So they covered their heads, and the lower part of their faces, with long strips of cloth, wound round and round. Men's styles looked rather like a **turban**, with a wide cloth strip protecting the mouth and nose. Women's styles were simpler, rather like shaws, and covered the whole face.

Caps and crowns

In West Africa, short, close-cropped hairstyles were popular among men and some women. Caps and head-ties were for ordinary people. Powerful West African kings and queens wore elaborate crowns and headdresses made of coral or colourful beads. Some crowns displayed portraits of royal ancestors; others made royal wearers look taller, and grander, than ordinary people.

A statue of Queen Inyang Inyang, from Benin, Nigeria, circa 1610 - 1620.

Married beauty

In many parts of Africa, young, unmarried girls went bare-headed. Covering the hair was a sign of married status. In regions where fine cloth was produced, especially West Africa, married women traditionally wore head-wraps or head-ties. These were large squares or long lengths of patterned fabric, folded and tied in pleasing arrangements. Simple wraps were worn by ordinary women. High, wide, complicated head-ties were a sign of wealth and status. They were worn by women who did little manual work.

An elaborate head-tie worn by a women from Algeria.

Signs of belonging

Many hats were worn, by men and women, to display their membership of one particular group. Sometimes, headgear was a sign of tribal or national identity. For example, the Herero women of Namibia wore high, wide hats, called 'duk', made of tightly-wrapped cloth. Sometimes, headgear displayed rank or bravery. Warriors from the Zulu people of South Africa wore plumes of ostrich feathers, and Masai warriors (now in Kenya) coloured their hair with orange-coloured mud and arranged it in plaits. Often, headdresses were an important part of ceremonial costumes, worn by masked dancers and priests.

Why were women's head-wraps useful, as well as attractive?

They cushioned the head when carrying heavy loads.

Herero women from Namibia in traditional duk hats.

EARLY AMERICAS

The continent of North and South America covers a vast area, with many different climate zones and environments. Native peoples living there developed a wide range of headgear, designed to suit local conditions and using local materials.

In the Cold

In the frozen Arctic, the Inuit and Aleut peoples made cosy hooded parkas and anoraks from seal-skin and fox fur. In tropical Central America, Maya people created headdresses out of brightly-coloured cloth, skilfully woven from local plant fibres and decorated with embroidery. In the high Andes mountains of South America, Inca craft-workers spun and wove soft, warm llama fleece to make hats with earflaps for protection against frostbite.

Fantastic Feathers

Feathers were used to make ceremonial headgear in many parts of North and South America. Usually, there were strict laws about who could wear them. The finest feathers were reserved for royal rulers. In Mexico, Aztec artists also showed them in headdresses worn by gods. Feathers were also awarded – rather like medals – to brave warriors.

This musician from Peru is wearing a modern version of ancient Inca hat design.

North American Indian style

Different tribes decorated their heads in very different ways. Some North American warriors shaved their heads, or left just a strip of long hair standing (this was later called a "Mohican"). Central American women arranged their hair on either side of their face in circular '**squash-blossom**' shapes,or pinned braids on top their heads to create 'horns'.

Chief Keokuk of the Sauk Indians sporting a "Mohican".

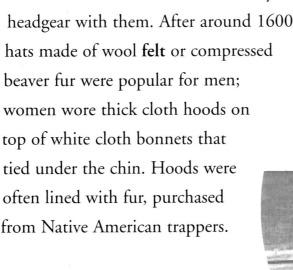

This warrior from a Native American tribe is wearing a headdress of red feathers.

How many birds were killed to make an Aztec feather headdress?

At least a hundred.

European settlers

After 1492, European explorers and settlers arrived in America. They brought European headgear with them. After around 1600, tall black hats made of wool **felt** or compressed beaver fur were popular for men; women wore thick cloth hoods on top of white cloth bonnets that tied under the chin. Hoods were often lined with fur, purchased from Native American trappers.

Beaver hats provided protection against the elements for European settlers.

EUROPE 1500-1750

In Europe, the years from 1500 to 1750 were exciting, troubled times. Explorers brought new products from distant lands; scholars, preachers and artists challenged old ideas. Headgear became some of the richest ever seen in Europe.

A group of Tudor boys dressed in bonnets.

Bonnets

Bonnets (wide flat **caps** without peaks), first worn by scholars and their pupils, were chosen by many fashionable men. But their caps were made of rich black silk velvet, and trimmed with imported feathers or pearls.

Headband designs

Fashionable women copied styles worn by powerful queens and princesses. The 'French hood' (a crescent-shape jewelled **cap** worn on top of a bag-like hood which covered most of the hair) was popular throughout Europe, so were neck ruffs – wide bands of pleated linen that originated in Spain. These framed the face, and were also worn by men. Poor people could not afford these fancy fashions; men wore woollen bonnets, women wore headscarves and shawls.

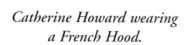

Catherine Howard wearing a French Hood.

A group of English men, ca. 1610, wearing typical wide-brimmed hats.

Post 1620

Around 1620, styles changed. Fashionable men and women wore long **ringlets** tumbling over their shoulders, and wide- brimmed hats of **felt**, beaver hair or leather. But strict Protestants (sometimes called Puritans) believed that frivolous styles were ungodly. Puritan men had close-cropped hair; Puritan women wore neat buns and plain white linen **caps**.

What is a more common name for a Chaperon?

A French Hood.

Post 1680

By around 1680, natural hair was replaced by long curled wigs. Men topped these with big tricorne (three-cornered) hats; women wore 'frontlets', lace headdresses stiffened by wire, with trailing ribbons, called 'lappets'. By around 1750, women's wigs had become outrageously high. They were padded with wool and decorated with flowers and feathers. In contrast, men's wigs were smaller, with neat short curls and a little pony-tail, called a 'queue'.

A 17th century illustration of a wealthy woman wearing a tricome.

23

WESTERN WORLD 1750~1900

Between 1750 and 1900, the western world – Europe, America, and some European colonies – changed more quickly than ever before. New styles were mass produced and publicised by the world's first fashion magazines, printed in France. Worker's hats remained plain and practical.

A selection of 'Romantic' style hats, dating from the 1850s.

Greek influence

From around 1780-1810, fashions were based on Ancient Greek designs. Men and women mostly went bare headed. Men had short, curled hair; women also cut their hair, or wore long locks upswept, in Greek style.

New Romantics

By 1820, new 'Romantic' fashions were in vogue for women. These featured shady 'picture' hats, or **bonnets** with wide **brims** that hid most of the wearer's face. Underneath, hair was tied back neatly into a bun. From around 1870, big **bonnets** were replaced by small dainty hats, worn tilting forwards. This made room for elaborate hairstyles with chignons or **ringlets** at the back.

Children were dressed like miniature adults. This girl is wearing a large straw picture hat, tied with a wide ribbon.

24

Men's Fashion

Around 1850, many new hat styles were introduced for men. A hard, dome-shaped, narrow-brimmed felt hat, became very popular. It was named after its designer, William Bowler. (In the USA, it was known as a 'Derby'.) Other new styles included a light, flat-crowned straw 'boater', for summertime wear, and a warm, wide brimmed soft felt hat, named after the town where it was first made: Homburg, in Germany. Men's hair was short and neat, but long, bushy side-whiskers were very fashionable.

*The **bowler** hat became the traditional headwear of London businessmen.*

In the USA

In the USA, new hats were designed to meet new working conditions. Trappers and huntsmen in the northern woods wore fur caps, often decorated with animal tails. Cowboys riding across hot, dusty prairies wore cool wide-brimmed, high-crowned stetsons. Housewives and women farm workers shaded their faces with big cotton sun-bonnets.

A selection of cowboy hats. These iconic hats kept cowboys cool during their working days.

25

Late 19th century styles remained popular at the start of the 20th century. Women's hats were still small, highly decorated and impractical; masses of waving, upswept hair were still seen as the female 'crowning glory'. Men's **top hats**, bowlers and homburgs remained in vogue, together with sporting styles, such as the 'deerstalker' **cap** and the jaunty **felt** hat.

World War 1

The start of World War I in 1914 changed fashions – for ever. Men wore uniform hats, or practical caps and helmets. Women wore neat, modest hats - or headgear linked to their wartime duties, such as nurses caps and veils, or headscarves and hairnets for work in weapons factories.

GRADUATE NURSES
YOUR COUNTRY NEEDS YOU

This WW1 recruiting poster shows a nurse in a cap.

Cloche hats of the 1920s were plain, simple and easy to wear. They would only fit over short hairstyles

The Cloche hat

After the war ended in 1918, women refused to return to their earlier way of life - or style of clothing. They cut their hair and experimented with the world's first 'perms' (permanent waves). They wore tight-fitting 'cloche' (bell-shaped) hats with tiny **brims**, pulled low down over the face.

Menswear

Flat cloth caps – sometimes large and baggy – were still popular with working men, and for playing sports such as golf. For daytime wear, country men also wore smart tweed caps. City-dwellers chose a soft, wide-brimmed felt hat, called a **Trilby** or a **Fedora** for informal wear, but smart businessmen preferred a **bowler hat** or very formal top hat.

The flat cap was worn by people of all classes and a variety of sportsmen around the world.

What was an opera hat?

A collapsible top hat.

World War II

A second terrible World War, from 1939-1945, saw men and women wearing uniform headgear. Off-duty, choice of hats was limited by severe shortages of fabric and trimmings. Styles were small, neat, and inspired by uniforms.

Men and women who joined the US aurfirce during World War II wore camouflaged helmets as part of their uniform.

27

WESTERN WORLD 1950-2000

The late 20th century was the first time – for thousands of years – when most men and women in the Western world did not wear hats as part of their everyday clothing. But for several years after the end of World War II in 1945, hats continued to be part of formal dress for men and women.

Special occasions

Older people wore them for special occasions such as weddings and funerals, and for attending Church services. Women's hat designs varied, from tiny 'pillboxes' to elaborate floral styles. Men's styles remained largely unchanged from earlier in the century.

*A model wears a 1960s-style **pillbox** hat as part of a wedding outfit. 1998.*

Out of Fashion?

But new technology – such as central heating and warm, comfortable car travel – made hats unnecessary as protection from bad weather. And new ideas made hats unfashionable, especially among the young. They said hats were out-of-date, silly and unattractive. To them, hats symbolised neatness, order, rank, and inequality.

Trendy cars made the concept of hat wearing unfashionable.

Changing hairstyles

Hairstyles remained important, however. From the 1960s, waist-length flowing hair (for men as well as women) mocked neat, tidy 1940s fashions. Often, it was dyed with henna imported from India. Bushy 'Afro' curls and dreadlocks were a way for people of African descent to display pride in their identity, and campaign for equality.

Rastafarian men grew long dreadlocks and wore knitted 'Tams' to show that they were followers of the religion. Tams can hold a mass of dreadlocks.

Hats for Work

The workplace was the only area of life where hats were worn more often. New   designed to protect workers, and new materials such as shatterproof plastics, led to the creation of improved safety headgear. Astronauts taking part in United States and Soviet Russian space exploration flights relied on specially-designed helmets to survive beyond the Earth's atmosphere.

What did the Apollo 11 crew smell when they took off their space helmets?

Moondust! NASA scientists believed that this was very explosive too!

Space helmets supplied astronauts with air to breathe. They also removed waste products.

GLOBAL STYLES TODAY

Today, in the early years of the 21st century, fashions have become global. TV, the Internet and other electronic devices take only seconds to transmit images of the latest styles all round the word. International corporations have factories making designs in many different countries, and sell them wherever they can find customers.

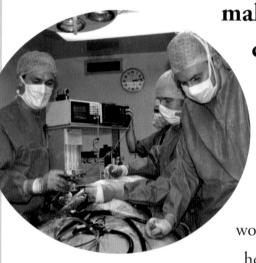

Hospital surgeons wear surgical masks and hairnets to keep the surgery free of germs.

Workers headgear

Following 20th century fashions, many men, women and children never wear a hat. However, headgear is still worn by many workers. Hospital staff wear **caps**, masks and hairnets to keep their workplace clean. Labourers, police, firemen, and soldiers all wear reinforced headgear. Tourists visiting hot, sunny countries are urged to protect their skin with large shady hats, as well as sunscreen.

Sport and leisure

Professional sports stars wear strong helmets decorated with team colours and sponsors' logos. Other sportswear styles, such as peaked baseball caps or pull-on knitted hats, are popular leisure wear, especially for young people. Like hooded tops, worn by gang members, they are a fashion statement and a sign of belonging.

A skateboarder wearing a protective helmet while executing a dramatic jump.

Religion

For people following older traditions, hats are still important. Many Jewish men choose to wear a Yarmulka (**skull-cap**) as a sign of respect for God. Muslim women and girls wear several different styles of head-covering – collectively called **hijab** (modest dress) - so do many Sikh and Muslim men. Elaborate headscarves and braided hairstyles are valued African traditions.

Men belonging to the Orthodox Hassidic Jewish community, founded in the 18th century, wear wide black hats.

What is the most popular hat in the world today?

The baseball cap.

High Fashion

Some men and women choose to wear hats simply because they like them, or make them feel good. Top fashion designers still dress supermodels in hats at yearly fashion shows. And some of the world's most famous people choose spectacular hats for important public appearances.

*A model with a trendy cord baggy flat **cap**, pictured in 2005.*

boater Hat made of stiff, plaited straw with a flat, shallow crown and a narrow brim.

bonnet (men) EITHER A baggy cap, with or without a brim.

bonnet (women) A hood-shaped hat, often with a frilled or lace-trimmed brim, that fastens under the chin.

bowler Hat with a narrow curved brim and a hard, dome-shaped crown. Also known as a derby.

brim The outer edge of a hat.

cap (men) EITHER a small, neat hat without a brim OR hat shaped like an upturned bowl, with a stiff peak attached.

cap (women) EITHER a small neat hat without a brim OR a small bonnet, made of lace or another thin, delicate white material.

chignon Long hair arranged in a twist or loose knot, and pinned up at the back of the head.

crown The part of a hat which covers the top of the head.

deerstalker Cap made of thick warm cloth, with flaps to cover the ears.

derby Hat with a narrow curved brim and a hard, dome-shaped crown. Also known as a bowler.

diadem Decorative headband.

fedora Soft felt hat with a wide brim. Also known as a trilby.

felt Thick cloth made of boiled, compressed wool or animal hair.

gable Pointed end of a roof. Also used to describe a headdress worn by women in 16th century Europe.

garland Circle of leaves or flowers.

hijab Modest dress worn by Muslims. Often used to describe a headscarf worn by women.

homburg Soft felt hat for men, first made in Homburg, Germany.

hoplite Citizen foot-soldier in Ancient Greece.

kammuri Tall black hat, worn by the high-ranking men in Japan.

keffiyah Cloth-headdress worn in Arab countries of North Africa and the Middle East.

lattice Criss-cross framework or network.

lock Trailing strand of hair.

nemes Striped cloth headdress, worn in Ancient Egypt.

pesatos Wide-brimmed leather hat worn in Ancient Greece.

pharaohs Kings of Ancient Egypt.

picture hat Woman's hat with a wide soft brim that frames the face. Often decorated with flowers and ribbons.

pillbox Small round, flat-topped hat without a brim. Named after the little cardboard boxes formerly used to contain pills.

pschent Double crown, worn by pharaohs of Ancient Egypt.

ringlets Long, tight, trailing curls.

squash-blossom The big, wide-open flowers of plants belonging to the squash (pumpkin) family.

tam A loose, baggy cap, often made of knitted fabric, worn by followers of the Rastafarian religion. (could add: The word is a short form of 'Tam O'Shanter' – the hero of a famous poem by Scots author, Robert Burns. The large, baggy bonnets (caps) worn by Scots men in the 19th century were nicknamed 'Tam O'Shanters, after the poem.)

tarboosh Cone shaped hat, traditionally worn in Turkey.

top hat Man's hat with a very tall, cylindrical crown. Usually made of black silk.

trilby Soft felt hat with a wide brim. Also known as a fedora.

turban A long strip of cloth wound round the head. Worn by men in Asia, and by male followers of the Sikh religion.

uraeus A cobra, head raised and ready to strike. A symbol of kingship and divine protection in Ancient Egypt.

Visigoths Tribes from north Europe who migrated to Italy and Spain soon after AD 500.

visor Face-covering. Part of a battle-helmet or other protective headgear.

Yarmulka Skull-cap worn by Jewish men.